Faith Blossoms and Honey Bees

Dear "Daddy,"
You created the heavens and the earth. Here is a story for you and your children. I hope it brings some of your heaven down here to our earth.

Joe Florio

WestBow Press books may be ordered through booksellers or by contacting:

WestBow Press
A Division of Thomas Nelson & Zondervan
1663 Liberty Drive
Bloomington, IN 47403
www.westbowpress.com
1 (866) 928-1240

ISBN: 978-1-5127-4730-0 (sc)
ISBN: 978-1-5127-4729-4 (e)

Library of Congress Control Number: 2016910380

Print information available on the last page.

WestBow Press rev. date: 07/19/2016

WESTBOW
PRESS®
A DIVISION OF THOMAS NELSON
& ZONDERVAN

This is a story about faith.

FAITH

Do you know what faith is?

Can you see it? Can you touch it?

Faith is confidence
or trust in a person or thing.

Faith is believing in
something you can't see.

Faith is something that grows
in our lives.

The Bible talks a lot about faith. It says... "What good is it, brothers and sisters, if you say you have faith but don't show it in your actions?" ~ James 2:14

Faith is special like a flower and our actions are like a worker bee. Now faith is so special, if it were a flower, it would be a blossom. What is a blossom?

A blossom is colorful and beautiful. It smells nice like perfume. Deep inside is sweet nectar that bees like to bring back to their hive.

A blossom is a very special flower
because this special flower
can make fruit.

There are all kinds
of blossoms.

There are apple blossoms, orange blossoms, pear blossoms, strawberry blossoms and even banana blossoms, to name just a few!

Let's see how a blossom makes fruit.
Bees are very busy searching
for sweet nectar for their
food. They are attracted by
the colors and sweet smell
of the blossoms.

They go from flower to flower collecting nectar. Also in the flower is a yellow powder called pollen. When busy bees go from flower to flower they bring some pollen along with them.

When pollen is added to the blossom the blossom slowly turns into something much greater than before!

Now a blossom all by itself is beautiful.

But without the work of a bee it only lasts a short time. After a week or two it withers away and dies and that's the end of it.

So busy bees are very important, because when they add their work to a flower ...

special things
start to happen!

The blossom flower now starts to change. It slowly creates something much bigger and better. It grows into beautiful fruit - apples, oranges, peaches, pears. This fruit lasts and lasts!

We eat it and it nourishes our bodies.

Our faith that we have in Jesus is special and beautiful, like a blossom.

When we use our gifts and add good deeds to our faith, beautiful things begin to happen and grow around us.

What is meant by good deeds? Good deeds are special things that we do for others! One good deed is caring for someone you don't know so well and treating them like they were close family.

It's easy to care about close friends and family - anyone can do that. **But what about that kid in school who eats lunch alone?**

Or how about that elderly neighbor down the block, the one you hardly ever see outside?

And what about that family across town whose house got flooded out?

Caring for them, spending time with them, working with them - that is something different. That kind of action is special!

That kind of action is LOVE! Love in action speaks louder than any words!

Think about this ...

If you were a tree... say you were a tree of faith, would your branches be empty?

Or would your faith tree have branches full of fruit?

What would your fruit look like? Is your fruit colorful and bright, like kindness? - Kindness like calling that lonely kid over to your lunch table?

Or is your fruit sweet and juicy, like caring? -
Caring enough to bring cookies with your parents
to that elderly neighbor on your street?

Or is your fruit packed with vitamins and energy? - Like helping a family in need across town?

So don't let your special flowers wither away and die.

Instead of keeping your faith all to yourself, add work to it just like a busy bee does and watch how things grow!

Add work offered up to the Lord. Love one another. Really love one another!

Make a difference in someone else's life and you will bear amazing fruit that lasts and lasts!

CPSIA information can be obtained at www.ICGtesting.com
Printed in the USA
BVOW05s1921300816

460578BV00005B/7/P